First published in 2023 by Comodo Publications.

Copyright © 2023 by Jason Gardner

Written by Jason Gardner

ISBN 978-1-9161107-2-4

For permission requests, please contact:
Jason Gardner 29 Knighton Road, Redhill, Surrey RH1 6EH

Acknowledgements

To Alison Platt, Caroline Conder, Christine Gellender-Mills, Fiona Barlow, Gail Bennett, Henri Monier-Williams, Julia Nash, Karen Murphy, Kerry Reichelt, Nicola Tate, Sophie Greene, your encouraging comments on my poems ignited my passion for writing and propelled the development of this project.

Thank you for your invaluable support.

Jason Gardner

Thank you for picking up this book! I am thrilled to inform you that your purchase will make a significant difference in the lives of many individuals and animals through the support of the following charitable organisations and not-for-profit community interest company:

1. **In the Company of Horses CIC** (Company number: 14288234): By supporting this organisation, you are contributing to their mission of promoting the therapeutic benefits of horses and equine-assisted activities for individuals with physical, emotional, or cognitive challenges.

2. **The Diamond Centre Charity** (Charity number: 1045970): Your contribution to this charity enables them to provide therapeutic horse riding sessions and equine-based activities for children and adults with disabilities, empowering them to develop confidence, strength, and independence.

3. **Friends of Luccombe Hub** (Charity number: 1188184): Through your generosity, you are helping this charity create a vibrant community hub, offering support, activities, and services for individuals of all ages, fostering a sense of belonging and social connection.

4. **Redwings Horse Sanctuary** (Charity number: 1068911): The funds raised from this book's sales will directly support Redwings Horse Sanctuary in their mission to provide a safe haven for neglected, abandoned, and mistreated horses, ensuring they receive the care and rehabilitation they desperately need.

5. **The Horse Trust** (Charity number: 231748): Your purchase contributes to The Horse Trust's vital work of providing retirement and sanctuary for working horses, as well as funding veterinary research and education programs to improve equine welfare.

By supporting these incredible organisations, you are joining a community of compassionate individuals who believe in the transformative power of horses and the importance of creating inclusive and caring communities. Your contribution truly makes a difference, and we are immensely grateful for your support.

Thank you for being a part of this meaningful journey.

Warmest regards, *Jason Gardner*

FRIENDS OF LUCCOMBE HUB

REDWINGS
HORSE SANCTUARY

The Horse Trust
Advancing Excellence
in Equine Care

INTRODUCTION

Poetry Galloping Through the Spirit of Horses

In the captivating realm where humans and horses forge an unbreakable bond, I have discovered a fountain of inspiration. "Poetry Galloping Through the Spirit of Horses" is a collection of poems that offers a heartfelt glimpse into my equestrian world—a world that has touched my soul and beckons me to share its wonders.

It all began with a poem—an ode to a dear friend whose young horse was lost too soon. As I sought solace in the power of words, my offering resonated with the equestrian community, igniting a flame within me. Encouraged by friends, I embarked on a poetic journey that now unfolds within these pages.

Each poem weaves together experiences, anecdotes, and reflections on the horses who have graced my life and those I have had the privilege to work with. From the spirited gallop across sun-drenched meadows to the gentle sway of a horse's head, every stride holds magic, captured by my pen.

In this equestrian realm, horses are more than companions—they are friends, confidants, and kindred spirits. They teach us patience, resilience, and the art of listening. Through their eyes, we glimpse our own humanity, finding solace and unity.

Immerse yourself in these verses, joining me on a journey of exploration. Marvel at the majesty of these noble creatures, their captivating presence, and the emotions they evoke. May these poems not only illuminate the equestrian world but touch your heart, bridging our shared love for horses and the beauty of words.

Note: In the poetic verses dedicated to my horse, his name "Ximen" should be pronounced as "Zimen." By replacing the "X" with a "Z" sound, we can create a harmonious flow that captures the essence of my equine companion.

v

Contents

Harmony Unbridled
Sonnet

In fields of grace, where mighty spirits dwell,
A dance unfolds with strength and harmony.
With hooves that pound, they weave a tale to tell,
Of partnership and trust in unity.

Their noble souls, a mirror to our own,
As sweat and toil unite our paths as one.
With gentle touch and whispers softly sown,
We forge a bond that cannot be undone.

Their power humbles, yet they offer grace,
A gentle nudge, a flicker in their eye.
They teach us patience, in their steady pace,
And with their wisdom, doubts and fears defy.

Oh, working with these creatures, proud and grand,
A gift bestowed upon the fortunate hand.

Politically Correct

In a world where horses roam free,
A tale unfolds of a politically correct being, you see.
With hooves of grace and a mane so fine,
This horse transcends boundaries, oh so divine!

No need for colours, it's chromatically diverse,
A rainbow-coated beauty, what a universe!
Inclusive neighs, it greets all with glee,
No discrimination, from stable to field, you see.

Its neighs are gender-neutral, inclusive in sound,
Supporting all pronouns, no boundaries to be found.
No bias for their breed or height,
Equal treatment for all, whether dark or light.

This horse refuses to trot with political strife,
Unifying bridles, erasing divisions from life.
Whether left or right, it takes a neutral stance,
Galloping toward harmony, a harmonious dance.

Politically correct, this horse does embrace,
With humour and love, filling every space.
So let's ride together, on this horse so grand,
Promoting laughter and unity across the land!

Buster, Ximen, Donald and Eddy

for Christine Gellender-Mills

Once upon a time, in a green meadow beyond the clouds,
Two Highland Ponies, Donald and Eddy, stood proud.
Looking down upon their old friend, Buster, they did see,
With his new companion, Ximen, happy and free.

Years ago, Donald and Eddy were by Buster's side,
Their friendship was a bond that would never subside.
Now as spirits above, they watched with delight,
Seeing Buster and Ximen, a joyful sight.

In the heavens, Donald and Eddy observed with care,
As Buster and Ximen grazed, a perfect pair.
Through fields they galloped, exploring far and wide,
Buster guided Ximen with wisdom and pride.

One day, as the ponies rested in the meadow's embrace,
Donald and Eddy decided to reveal their celestial grace.
Shining spirits, with coats gleaming and wings so grand,
They appeared to their friends, a magical band.

"Hello, old friend," Donald said, nuzzling Buster dear,
Buster's heart filled with warmth, without any fear.
"It's so good to see you," Buster said with glee,
"And this is Ximen, who means the world to me."

Eddy greeted Ximen with kindness in his eyes,
"We're pleased to meet you, under these glorious skies.
Take care of our friend, as you've done so well,
Together, you make a story we love to tell."

The four ponies grazed together, sharing their tales,
Of past and present, of triumphs and trails.
Donald and Eddy shared memories from afar,
While Buster and Ximen dreamed of what lay under the stars.

As the sun began to set, casting hues in the sky,
Donald and Eddy bid their friends goodbye.
They promised to visit again, to watch from above,
Guarding Buster and Ximen with unwavering love.

Buster and Ximen knew they were never alone,
Their friendship a treasure, forever known.
In the meadow, they roamed, their spirits alive,
With two guardian angels, their hearts would thrive.

And so, the days passed, in the meadow so wide,
Buster and Ximen, side by side.
With the spirits of Donald and Eddy, a bond so true,
They knew their friendship would forever renew.

Once upon a time, in a green meadow beyond the clouds,
Two Highland Ponies found solace, amongst nature's shrouds.
With spirits as companions, their souls would never wane,
In that everlasting meadow, their friendship would remain.

Buster

for Joseph Gellender-Mills

In the meadows of Warlingham, where the bridle paths wind,
There lives a small pony, the friendliest of its kind.
His name is Buster, a Shetland so fine,
With a heart full of joy and a spirit so benign.

Buster ambles along with a confident stride,
His hooves gentle and nimble, with grace as his guide.
He greets every creature he meets on his way,
With a nudge and a whinny, making their worries allay.

But oh, the big horses, they tremble in fear,
At the sight of our Buster, so small and so dear.
With snorts and wide eyes, they want to flee,
Not knowing Buster's intentions, so happy and carefree.

Approaching them with a twinkle in his eye,
He nudges their noses, hoping they'd comply.
But the big ones, they shiver, their legs feeling weak,
Misunderstanding the kindness that Buster would seek.

They'd turn and they'd run, away from his charms,
Not realising Buster meant no harm.
Oh, poor Buster, with his head held low,
He watches them retreat, his friendly spirit aglow.

With his head held high, he continues his way,
Spreading joy and kindness, come what may.
He trots down the bridle paths, cheerful and bright,
Bringing smiles to all, under the golden sunlight.

For Buster knows deep inside, within his gentle soul,
That love conquers fears, making hearts whole.
So, let's remember dear Buster, the pony so grand,
A symbol of friendship, across the equestrian land.

For in Buster's presence, we find something rare,
A reminder to cherish the beauty we share.
The smallest acts of kindness shine so bright,
Make the world radiant, both day and night.

Stubborn Ximen's Dilemma

for Thomas and Jake Gardner

In his field, where the grass grows lush and green,
Lives my horse, the stubbornest you've seen.
Ximen is his name, a quirky fellow,
With a mind of his own, who can be so mellow!

He wanted to be caught, that much was clear,
But staying out in the field brought him cheer.
"Come here, Ximen, a ginger biscuit I bring!"
But he hesitated, pondering like a king.

To be caught or to graze, the choice was tough,
Ximen couldn't decide, it was just too much!
With longing eyes, he gazed at the treat,
But the field's allure was simply too sweet.

Buster, his Shetland Pony brother, nearby,
Waited patiently, giving Ximen a sigh.
"Come, my bro., let's go back to the stable,
The adventure awaits, we're ready and able!"

Ximen thought for a moment, his mind in a whirl,
Being in charge, making decisions, a tempting twirl.
But deep down, he knew, it was all just a sham,
For guidance and direction, he needs like a lamb.

So with a snort and a nudge from his friend,
Ximen surrendered, ready to amend.
He followed Buster, guided by his lead,
Hoping to satisfy his indecisive steed.

In the stable, they found comfort and rest,
With Ximen realising it was for the best.
No big decisions to make, just hay and straw,
He could relax, without a worry or flaw.

Oh, Ximen, the horse with a stubborn streak,
Yearning for control, yet finding it weak.
He taught us a lesson, a humorous tale,
Sometimes it's best to let others prevail.

Boundless Hooves

Pantoum

On horseback I ride across the land,
Hooves pounding the earth with rhythmic grace,
Wind whispers secrets through the flowing mane,
As freedom's spirit lifts my soul, unchained.

Hooves pounding the earth with rhythmic grace,
Through fields and forests, we forge our way,
As freedom's spirit lifts my soul, unchained,
A bond unbreakable, we proudly display.

Through fields and forests, we forge our way,
Gallop and canter, in perfect harmony,
A bond unbreakable, we proudly display,
Together we conquer, a timeless story.

Gallop and canter, in perfect harmony,
Exploring horizons, we know no bounds,
Together we conquer, a timeless story,
The horse and rider, forever renowned.

Exploring horizons, we know no bounds,
Wind whispers secrets through the flowing mane,
The horse and rider, forever renowned,
On horseback I ride across the land.

The Luccombe Hub

for Henri Monier-Williams

In the heart of Dorset, there lies a place,
A haven for young souls seeking solace and grace.
Where learning takes a different form, unique and rare,
The Luccombe Hub, a sanctuary of care.

Here, it's not about teaching, but focusing on growth,
Nurturing young minds that have faced hardship and loath.
For those who couldn't access mainstream's embrace,
Trauma, anxiety, and lack of social skills they face.

Within these walls, a haven of compassion blooms,
A place where judgment finds no room.
The children find solace in recognising their own hearts,
Discovering feelings, voicing anxieties, and playing their parts.

An atmosphere of understanding fills the air,
As emotions are unveiled, with tender hands, we share.
Their moods, their triggers, their inner storms,
Learned here are the skills to weather and transform.

With hands-on experiences and the outdoors as a guide,
They explore a world where healing resides.
A therapeutic embrace, like nature's gentle caress,
Empowers them to express and release, no less.

Art becomes a language, a medium to speak,
A canvas where their souls find solace and seek.
And through practical activities that build trust,
Their self-esteem and confidence rise from the dust.

Within these walls, there are no year groups or bounds,
Each student's journey, uniquely profound.
They delve into passions, following their desires,
Unleashing their potential, igniting their fires. ·

Led by their own choices, empowered they stand,
In a non-judgmental space, carefully planned.
A structure that nurtures, with unconditional regard,
Their hearts find guidance, their souls safely guarded.

At The Luccombe Hub, resilience finds its birth,
A sanctuary for minds seeking new worth.
Young souls blossom, like flowers in bloom,
Learning to navigate a world, sometimes marooned.

In Luccombe's haven, nature's harmony thrives,
Students and creatures, healing their lives.
With animals wounded, neglected and frail,
Compassion blooms, a heart-warming tale.

Horses, alpacas, sheep, and pigs they adore,
Through care and connection, scars heal and restore.
These gentle beings, survivors of strife,
Teach empathy, resilience, transforming life.

So let us celebrate this place of love and care,
Where learning takes flight in the open air.
The Luccombe Hub, a beacon shining bright,
Guiding young hearts to embrace their own light.

Kingsmead Equestrian Centre

for the horse care and yard teams

At Kingsmead Equestrian Centre, where hoofbeats dance,
A sanctuary of grace, horses enhance.
Within their herds, a vibrant mosaic unfolds,
Where equine spirits roam, as freedom beholds.

Behold in awe as their social symphony plays,
Galloping and grazing, untold tales ablaze.
For herd life is their cherished embrace,
In Kingsmead's haven, their noble space.

Majestic beings, each with a distinct soul,
Tailored work and care, their lives enfold.
With knowledge and pride, their needs we meet,
Vet, farrier, and dentist, ensuring their fleet.

From the tiniest pony, measuring eight hands high,
To the grandest steed, reaching for the sky.
Steady cobs amble, carrying dreams on their back,
Energetic warmbloods, power they never lack.

In Kingsmead's equestrian symphony divine,
A harmonious blend, where horses align.
Come, witness their grace, as they freely roam,
Where equine spirits find solace and home.

Billy's Slumber

for Nicola Tate

Today, dear Billy seeks solace and rest,
A peaceful afternoon, a slumber he's blessed.
Within his cosy stable, he finds his repose,
The sweet scent of haylage, where tranquillity flows.

The sun casts its warmth, painting shadows on his coat,
As Billy dreams of adventures and landscapes remote.
His hooves twitch in rhythm with dreams deep and grand,
A whimsical journey through a magical land.

Yet as the time passes, the stable needs care,
The shavings and the mess call for someone to dare.
But Billy, unmoving, does not want to wake,
He pleads for more slumber, a wish he does make.

"Oh, dear friend," he murmurs, his voice a soft plea,
"Let my dreams continue, just a while longer, you see.
The stable can wait, for a moment of rest,
The beauty of slumber, I cherish it best."

So, let the stable wait, let the chores be delayed,
For Billy, our dear friend, in his dreams is conveyed.
In dreams, we find solace, in rest, we renew,
And Billy, dear Billy, we're grateful for you.

Celeste

for Fiona Barlow

In a land of rolling hills and fields of green,
Lived a horse named Celeste, the most majestic you've seen.
She was loved by all who cared for her with all their might,
And she knew that love, shining in her eyes so bright.

Celeste was the matriarch of the herd,
And watched over all who worked and visited, without a single word.
She was a gentle soul, with a heart of gold,
And her beauty and grace never grew old.

One day, much too soon, Celeste passed away,
Leaving all who knew her with heavy hearts to sway.
But the next day, a rainbow appeared in the sky,
And it felt like Celeste had come to say goodbye.

The rainbow was a symbol of her love and care,
A reminder that her spirit was always there.
Watching over her horse and human family with pride,
Guiding them through life, no matter where they reside.

Celeste's memory lives on, forever in their hearts,
Her gentle nature and kind spirit will never depart.
She may have left this world, but her love remains,
And it will always shine bright, like the rainbow's colourful stains.

Patch's Equine Magic

for Gail Bennett

Riding for the disabled, a symphony of dreams,
Where strength arises, where hope redeems.
Justin, on Patch, their bond so strong,
A partnership blooming, where dreams belong.

In the saddle's embrace, freedom awakes,
As worries dissolve and happiness takes.
Patch and Justin, a harmony so true,
Inspire hearts, with each stride they pursue.

With each gentle nudge, Patch's soul ignites,
A beacon of hope, amidst daunting heights.
Together they conquer life's daunting tasks,
Unyielding determination, no challenge masks.

In RDA's realm, a sanctuary divine,
Healing through hoofbeats, a moment so fine.
For in the saddle's refuge, miracles unfold,
Where horse and rider merge, a story yet untold.

So let us celebrate this magical ride,
Where courage and grace triumph side by side.
For Justin and Patch, their journey's just begun,
Unleashing the magic of riding, forever spun.

Gizmo

for Julia Nash

In a place of joy and sheer delight,
Resides a Shetland pony, a charming sight.
Gizmo is his name, a Shetland Grey,
At Kingsmead Equestrian Centre he finds his way.

With three pony pals, a merry band,
They trot and gallop across the land.
But Gizmo shines, a little equine prince,
With a heart full of joy that makes us wince.

Gizmo loves the children, oh so sweet,
Their little hands grooming him with care and treat.
With brushes and combs, they tend to his care,
And he'll sniff their pockets for treats to share.

At Kingsmead, the children come to play,
Giggles and smiles that brighten each day.
They hop on Gizmo for a pony ride,
Clip-clopping together, side by side.

Gizmo's hooves dance with glee,
As he carries them safely, wild and free.
Through green fields and paths so wide,
He's a trusty steed with a bouncy stride.

He's not just a pony, but a furry friend,
With a mischievous spirit that has no end.
He'll wiggle his ears and give a cheeky wink,
Bringing laughter to all, from the smallest to the brink.

The children adore him, oh, it shows,
With each passing day, their love for Gizmo grows.
They'll gather 'round him, a happy throng,
Singing songs and laughing all day long.

So if you're ever at Kingsmead's gate,
Look for Gizmo, a pony who's great.
He'll greet you with a nuzzle and a friendly smile,
Ready for adventure, mile after mile.

For Gizmo, the grey Shetland star,
With children around, he's never far.
At Kingsmead, a place of joy and glee,
Gizmo and his friends, where happiness runs free.

Twiggy's Tapestry of Kindness
for Sophie Greene

In fields embraced by gentle, swaying breeze,
Twiggy, my horse, stands tall with graceful ease.
Whickering softly as I stroll her way,
Her voice of warmth, a heartfelt display.

On days I drive into her view, she nods her head,
With a spirited energy, she's lovingly bred.
Her steadfast loyalty, an unwavering light,
A noble companion, a treasure shining bright.

Through fields and trails, she tries her best,
Her little heart, never shying from the test.
No matter what I ask, she gives her all,
A true partner, she heeds my every call.

In whispers, she shares when things aren't right,
Knowing I'll listen, her trust takes flight.
No need to shout, for I understand her plight,
In her silent language, our bond takes flight.

Mischievous moments, she can't resist,
Unzipping pockets, a playful twist.
Chattering her lips in whimsical glee,
Her joyful spirit sets our friendship free.

When I sit near her stable, brushing her legs,
She plays with my hair, a tender dance she begs.
Her gentle touch, a gesture filled with grace,
Creating harmony in this special place.

With her head, she nudges, a gentle push,
Seeking attention, in conversations hushed.
She yearns for connection, a moment's affection,
Her devotion shining through, without objection.

To every person and creature, she extends her love,
A friend to all, with a heart soaring above.
Her kindness transcends the boundaries of her kind,
Embracing the world with a gentle, open mind.

In the field, set free, she throws shapes with delight,
A spirited soul, embracing freedom's height.
Her radiant joy, a captivating sight,
A muse of dance, her spirit shining bright.

When new or ailing, she assumes a motherly grace,
Nurturing with tenderness, fear she'll erase.
A comforting presence, a guardian so dear,
Her gentle nature, a solace for souls held near.

With quirkiness and whimsy, she adorns her air,
A mummy's girl, a bond so loving and rare.
But kindness, above all, defines her core,
A beacon of compassion, making spirits soar.

So let us celebrate Twiggy, our dear equine friend,
Whose presence in our lives we'll cherish, without end.
With every whicker and nod, a tapestry she's spun,
Threads of love, trust, and friendship, forever to be one.

A Poetic Journey into Basic Horse Care

for hard-working Grooms everywhere

In the place where hooves gracefully prance,
A tale of care and love begins to dance.
With gentle strokes and tender embrace,
Basic horse care, a harmonious chase.

Shelter stands tall, a haven from the storm,
Where equine souls find solace, safe and warm.
Stables of peace, where the winds may not roam,
Shielding from nature's wrath, a cherished home.

Feeding the essence of life's grand display,
Nourishing horses, each and every day.
Forage of quality, a feast to bestow,
Fuelling their spirits, letting vitality grow.

Water, the elixir, a lifeline so pure,
Quenching their thirst, an endless allure.
Glistening troughs, where liquid diamonds gleam,
Sustaining their spirits, like a flowing dream.

Grooming, a ritual of tender devotion,
Caressing their coats, with heartfelt emotion.
Removing the dust and remnants of the day,
Unveiling their beauty, like the sun's golden ray.

Hooves, the foundation of strength and grace,
Trimmed with care, in a rhythmic embrace.
Balanced and sound, they stride with pride,
Paths made smooth, where their spirits reside.

Exercise and turnout, a dance with the earth,
Freedom to roam, where freedom finds its worth.
Grazing on pastures, where friendship is found,
Communion of souls, their hearts so profound.

Veterinary care, a guardian's touch,
Preventing ailments that burden too much.
Vaccines and deworming, guardians of health,
A vigilant watch, preserving equine wealth.

Companionship, a gift they hold dear,
The company of friends, forever near.
Galloping together, in fields wide and free,
Their spirits entwined, like branches of a tree.

In this realm of love, a bond so pure,
Basic horse care, an ode to endure.
For those who tend with hearts full of care,
Horses thrive, in a world beyond compare.

Cleaning Water Buckets
my obsession!

In the world of horses, where health is prime,
Cleaning their water buckets is no small-time.
These majestic creatures, prone to infection,
Are at risk if we neglect this protection.

Dirty buckets can play host to germs galore,
And make our equine friends feel awfully sore.
Neglected buckets, a bacterial spree,
Diseases unleashed, what a sight to see!

A slimy biofilm, like a slippery dance floor,
Forms on the surface, oh what a bore!
It's a haven for pathogens, lurking within,
Ready to make our noble steeds feel thin.

Not only that, but oh, what a shame,
Dirty buckets can ruin water's good name.
The taste and the smell, it becomes quite a fuss,
Leaving horses parched and rather nonplus.

In hot weather and during intense rides,
Dehydration becomes a health concern that hides.
Without clean water, they're left high and dry,
Their spirits wilt, and they can't help but sigh.

So, to keep our trusty companions aglow,
Let's clean their buckets, and off we go!
Disinfect and scrub, make them shine anew,
Fresh water awaits, ensuring health through and through.

By cleaning their buckets, we show our affection,
Preventing diseases and ensuring their protection.
Hydration intact, their well-being on track,
Happy horses prance with a lively knack.

Me 'orse and me

for Pete Gardner

On me jodhpurs, I mount me geezer,
Holdin' reins tight like a crowd-pleaser.
Whippin' 'round the track, with speed and grace,
Me 'orse and me, in sync, we embrace.

Tally-ho, we're off, in full gallop we go,
Leadin' the pack, puttin' on a show.
Dodgin' puddles, jumpin' gates, no sweat,
Me trusty steed and me, a duo you won't forget.

In the saddle, me cockney charm's unleashed,
Ridin' tall, me spirit can't be breached.
Stirrups jinglin', rhythm never missin',
This 'orseback adventure, pure cockney blissin'.

My Steed and I

Adorned in my jodhpurs, I graciously mount my noble companion,
Gently grasping the reins, as if performing for an adoring congregation.
Swiftly manoeuvring around the course, with a finesse and celerity,
My steed and I, in perfect unison, share a moment of harmony.

Tally-ho, our departure commences, in a magnificent canter we embark,
Leading the ensemble, captivating the audience, igniting a spark.
Navigating the obstacles with poise, nary a bead of perspiration to shed,
My loyal equine partner and I, an indelible duo, not soon to be misread.

Within the saddle, my refined charisma blossoms unrestrained,
Elevated in stature, my spirit invincible, steadfastly maintained.
As the stirrups emit a delightful symphony, rhythm never wavering,
This equestrian escapade, an embodiment of euphoria,
an enrapturing offering.

The Heartbeat of a Great Horse Riding Instructor
for those skilled, passionate, patient, experienced & dedicated.

In the enchanting world where horses and riders connect,
There thrives a unique symphony of mutual respect.
Within this dance, a skilled instructor takes the lead,
Nurturing dreams and fulfilling every rider's need.

Their vast knowledge, a treasure trove of equestrian art,
Grounded in horsemanship, a blend of science and heart.
Understanding the ways of these magnificent creatures,
They share their wisdom, weaving stories as gifted teachers.

Their words, like melodies, flow with clarity and grace,
Crafting a harmony that envelops every learning space.
From beginners taking their first timid strides,
To seasoned riders seeking new horizons to ride.

Safety is their foremost concern, an unwavering guide,
Protecting their students with expertise and pride.
From snug helmets to secure boots, they vigilantly ensure,
A sanctuary of reassurance, where riders can feel secure.

Their spirits ablaze with an unquenchable fire,
Passion for horses and teaching, their deep desire.
Their dedication knows no bounds, persistently they strive,
To ignite the same spark in every rider's soul, alive.

Adaptability is their secret weapon, a skill that they possess,
Tailoring their instruction to each individual's progress.
With patience and resourcefulness, challenges they meet,
Transforming obstacles into pathways, with steadfast feet.

Empathy flows through their veins, a comforting tide,
Supporting students with kindness, by their side.
They heal the fears, the doubts, and the wounds of the heart,
Creating a sanctuary where confidence can restart.

In this grand symphony, they conduct the ride,
Guiding souls to soar with untamed pride.
They sculpt riders' talents, unearthing their true art,
Leaving an indelible mark etched in every rider's heart.

In the enchanting world where horses and riders unite,
Their presence shines like stars, casting a guiding light.
The heartbeat of a great instructor echoes through the land,
A testament to their impact, crafted by a nurturing hand.

Haikus

Saddled aspirations,
Lessons taught, horse and rider,
Unison in stride.

Silent woodland path,
Horse's mane whispers through breeze,
Wild beauty embraced.

Tender touch and care,
Brushing coat, soothing whispers,
Horse's heart finds peace.

Meticulous hands,
Grooming grace, love in details,
Equine elegance.

Clerihews

Frankie Dettori, a jockey with flair,
Riding horses with style and care.
In the saddle, he's a true maestro,
Winning races wherever he may go.

Charlotte Dujardin, a dressage queen,
Gracefully riding, a sight to be seen.
With her horse, she forms a magical pair,
Equestrian talent beyond compare.

Steve Guerdat, a show jumping star,
Leaping high and clearing every bar.
With precision and skill, he conquers the course,
A champion rider, with unwavering force.

Roxanne Trunnell, Para-dressage delight,
With grace and determination, she takes flight.
Determined and strong, she rides with grace,
Inspiring hearts in the equestrian space.

For Sale

For Sale: The Horse with No Name, what a shame!
A scruffy, bad-tempered soul, with a not-so-charming fame.
If you seek a wild ride, full of surprises and distress,
This equine mystery is here to cause you nothing but stress!

With a coat so tangled, it hasn't seen a brush in years,
Grooming is an endeavour that's met with snorts and sneers.
Who needs a sleek appearance, all tidy and neat?
Embrace the "just rolled out of the pasture" look, let it be your treat!

No love for other animals or people does this horse possess,
He'd rather keep his distance, in solitude, his happiness.
So, saddle up and prepare for a lonely equestrian affair,
With a horse that couldn't care less, oh my, what a pair!

Loading onto a trailer? Well, that's a futile endeavour,
He'll play a game of hide-and-seek that'll last forever.
Persistence, bribery, and sweet talk, all in vain,
This horse won't be lured into that confined domain.

Spookiness is his expertise, a talent to behold,
A rustling leaf transforms into a monstrous stronghold.
Your heart will race, your hair will stand on end,
As this horse turns ordinary sights into a thrilling trend.

Visits from the vet, farrier, or dentist? Oh, how he hates!
They become his nemesis, a source of great debate.
Good luck persuading this equine rebel to cooperate,
As he battles the professionals with an attitude, oh, the fate!

Traffic becomes a challenge, a battleground of fear,
As passing cars ignite a panic that's oh so clear.
Hold onto your reins and pray for smooth passage,
With this horse, the road becomes a thrilling, nerve-wracking adage.

Leisurely hacks are a thing of the past, it seems,
For this horse, adventure is the stuff of dreams.
Whether alone or in company, chaos is his game,
So embrace the unpredictability, and revel in the fame!

But amidst all the troubles, let's not forget,
This horse has a face that's cute, no need to fret.
With adorable looks that tug at your heartstrings,
You may find yourself forgiving these equine misgivings.

So, if you're a glutton for punishment, a thrill-seeker at heart,
This horse is waiting, ready to tear your world apart.
A sense of humour, and patience, a must in this case,
As you embark on a journey filled with challenges to face.

Price? Well, it's a "steal" of a deal, that's for sure,
But be prepared for the trials that lie in store.
No refunds, no exchanges, no regrets, I must say,
This horse, with no name and an attitude, is here to stay!

Contact us now, if you dare take the leap,
Into a partnership that's unconventional, oh so deep.
May luck be your companion on this wild equine ride,
For with this horse, adventures await on every stride!

In the Company of Horses

for Caroline Conder, Patricia Harrod & Shaan Burton

In the company of horses, where hearts find solace,
ITCH, a noble endeavour, with purpose we embrace.
A not-for-profit venture, with a vision so clear,
At Kingsmead Equestrian Centre, their presence is near.

Amidst Warlingham's landscape, where beauty resides,
They offer accessible activities, where hope coincides.
Education, their guiding light, they strive to impart,
Teaching lessons beyond the saddle, reaching every heart.

Outreach riding, our offering, a gift so profound,
To those who seek solace, a safe haven they've found.
For those who would benefit, with hearts full of need,
Their horses extend healing, with love as their creed.

Beyond riding's confines, their purpose runs deep,
Incomprehensible treasures, secrets they keep.
For ITCH believes in the power to rebalance and recharge,
By connecting with horses, a pathway we enlarge.

In the realm of education and outreach they reside,
ITCH's remit, a beacon of support, far and wide.
Emotional, physical, and social well-being they seek,
Accessible and affordable, for the brave and the meek.

In the company of horses, a harmony so rare,
A tapestry woven with love and tender care.
ITCH and Kingsmead, champions of unity and grace,
Where healing and growth find their rightful place.

The Diamond Centre for Disabled Riders

At The Diamond Centre, where spirits alight,
A haven of joy, a beacon of light.
For disabled riders, young and old,
With horses and love, their stories unfold.

A registered charity, their noble cause,
To touch lives, and grant applause.
350 riders each passing week,
From three to seventy-five, strong and meek.

In the presence of horses, they find solace,
Mounted or unmounted, their dreams take flight.
Vaulting and driving, with skilled guide,
Instructors, volunteers, all by their side.

Physical strength, they steadily gain,
Sensory wonders, a vibrant terrain.
Education blooms, knowledge extends,
Communication flourishes, fences mend.

Laughter dances in every stride,
Each session a treasure, hearts open wide.
From riders to staff, a shared embrace,
Joy radiates, lighting up each face.

The Diamond Centre, a place of grace,
Where abilities triumph, challenges erase.
In the presence of horses, they find their way,
A sanctuary of hope, where smiles hold sway.

Clumsy Rider's Folly

There once was a rider quite absurd,
The worst in the land, or so I've heard.
A dozen bad habits, this rider possessed,
On horseback, they were simply a jest.

First, they'd mount with a reckless flair,
No grace or skill, just a stumble and swear.
Their stirrups too short, legs flailing about,
Like a drunken sailor, they'd wobble and shout.

Their reins, oh my, a tangled mess,
With a grip so loose, it caused much distress.
They'd pull left and right, without any clue,
Leaving their poor horse in quite a stew.

Next came the leaning, a sight to behold,
Off balance and slanted, they'd struggle to hold.
Their body contorted, in an awkward pose,
As if they were practising for circus shows.

They'd kick and kick, with heels like stone,
But their horse ignored them, left them alone.
No amount of urging could make it go,
It stood there, unimpressed, with a look of woe.

Their seat, oh dear, it was all askew,
Bouncing and bouncing, like they had no clue.
Their horse's back suffered, aching in pain,
Under the weight of this rider's disdain.

They'd forget their helmet, a crucial mistake,
A recipe for disaster, make no mistake.
Their hair in disarray, like a bird's nest,
With each jump and jolt, it looked quite distressed.

No patience had they, in training or guide,
Their horse would rebel, and rightly decide,
To give them a lesson, a humbling fall,
Perhaps then they'd learn, once and for all.

But despite their flaws, we couldn't help but smile,
For this rider's antics went on for miles.
A cautionary tale, a comedy show,
The worst horse rider the world did know.

There is no such thing as a bad horse

Some may whisper tales of horses gone bad,
Of aggression and mischief, driving humans mad,
But heed this truth, let wisdom take its course,
There is no such thing as a bad horse.

Within their hearts, strength intertwined,
Intelligence gleams, their brilliance defined,
Prey animals, cautious, ever aware,
Their instincts guide them, a vigilant affair.

Yet fear can ignite an untamed flame,
When threats arise, their composure maimed,
Behold the dance of fight or flight,
Their reactions, a testament to their plight.

But blame not the horse for its natural ways,
For these are the instincts time cannot erase,
Seek understanding, empathy's course,
And witness the transformation of a gentle force.

Inadequate guidance, a stumbling block,
Untrained, confused, their spirits may lock,
Clear communication, training's embrace,
A foundation built on patience and grace.

Handlers must learn to nurture their trust,
To listen, to guide, to adjust,
Failure lies not with the horse, but the hand,
A partnership faltered, yet hope can withstand.

Sometimes physical ailments take their toll,
A sore back, aching teeth, burdening the soul,
With care and healing, the clouds shall disperse,
Revealing the horse's true nature, a universe.

Individuality shines in each equine eye,
A spectrum of temperaments, none should decry,
Some exude warmth, with a spirit untamed,
Others tread softly, their essence unnamed.

But judge not their character by first sight,
For within their souls, depths of might,
In every horse, a story unfurls,
A canvas of uniqueness, a tapestry of pearls.

So remember, dear souls, as you ride your course,
There is no such thing as a bad horse,
With compassion and guidance, let love be the source,
Embrace the beauty, the spirit, the force.

REDWINGS
HORSE SANCTUARY

In fields of green, where hoofbeats play,
We hold a belief, guiding our way,
For every horse, pony, donkey, and mule,
A life of happiness, free from cruel.

From all corners of the UK's land,
We rescue those with fate in hand,
Abandoned, neglected, mistreated souls,
We offer refuge, where healing unfolds.

Redwings, a beacon, shining so bright,
The largest horse charity, in its might,
Over 2,000 creatures, in our care,
Supported by donations, love we share.

A safe haven we offer, a sanctuary true,
Where they can live, thrive, and renew,
Veterinary aid, a vital embrace,
Rehabilitation, a gentle grace.

Lifelong devotion, we pledge to bestow,
For these equine companions, so in need to grow,
But not just within our haven's domain,
We strive to educate, hearts to train.

We promote the care, protection we seek,
A haven for those with futures unique,
Rehoming those with dreams untold,
A chance for lives beyond our hold.

Through owners and generations, we impart,
The value of horse welfare, an enduring art,
For in the depths of compassion's gate,
Lies the beauty of these creatures, innate.

So let our mission resound loud and clear,
To cherish each equine, hold them dear,
For every horse, pony, donkey, and mule,
A happy, healthy life, our steadfast rule.

View Between the Ears

As I sit in the saddle, my vision sharp and clear,
Through woods and fields, a vibrant world appears.
The horse's ears become my window wide,
Nature's artwork revealed, on this joyful ride.

Sunlight filters through the leafy canopy,
Whispering tales and secrets just for me.
A canopy of green, nature's embrace,
As hooves dance on this enchanted space.

Tangled roots, like veins, pulse beneath our stride,
Earth's rhythm pulses, horse and rider side by side.
Wildflowers sway, a vivid mosaic,
Colours interwoven, nature's magic.

Between the ears, I glimpse the feathered flight,
Where birds compose their songs, with pure delight.
In blue skies, their freedom knows no bounds,
A mirrored reflection as our journey compounds.

Through the horse's eyes, I catch fleeting glance,
The creatures of the wild in nature's dance.
A deer, majestic, leaps with graceful might,
While rabbits scamper, hidden from my sight.

Oh, the wonders unfold as we journey as one,
On this grand adventure, under the warming sun.
Between the ears, a harmonious blend,
A rider's journey, with nature as my friend.

The Horse Trust

In eighteen eighty-six it began,
The Home of Rest for Horses, a noble plan,
To aid the weary workers of London's streets,
With shelter and solace, their tired hooves to treat.

For over a century, their mission held true,
A haven for horses, where love always grew,
Now known as The Horse Trust, a name so grand,
Symbolising their reach, across the land.

In Buckinghamshire, their home stands strong,
A sanctuary for horses, where they belong,
Over a hundred retired and rescued they keep,
Safe from the hardships they've known, buried deep.

And within those grounds, a centre does reside,
A beacon of knowledge, where expertise does guide,
Through research and training, they strive to improve,
Horse care and well-being, their goals they pursue.

Advice and guidance, to owners they lend,
Equine professionals, their knowledge they extend,
The Horse Trust, a symbol of compassion and grace,
A guardian for horses, in every time and space.

So let us celebrate this noble trust,
A sanctuary of hope, a legacy robust,
With open hearts, they offer a helping hand,
To the majestic creatures that roam this land.

Embrace the Journey
Acrostic poem

Harnessing the wind, we gallop with grace
On horseback, we embark on a thrilling chase
Roaming through meadows, a boundless space
Swift and agile, we gallop with great might,
Eternity in motion, a captivating sight.

Revel in the joy of horse riding's embrace
Invigorate your spirit, let it find its rightful place
Dwell in the beauty of landscapes, serene and secure
Ignite your passion for adventure's allure
Navigating trails with strength and affection
Galloping freely, we forge a connection

Amidst the wild, we find our escape
Daringly we ride, the thrill takes shape
Venturing forth, where freedom abounds
Equestrian spirits, unbridled and profound
Nature's wonders beckon, a call to explore
Timeless adventures, forever we'll adore
Unleashing our souls, as we gallop and glide
Revelling in the journey, side by side
Eager hearts ignite, with passion as our guide

Me 'orse, Soakin' in Storms

In the East End's gloomy fog, on my trusty nag I sit,
'Riding in the Barney Rubble,' ain't no time to quit.
Dodgin' the deluge, like a proper ol' pro,
Through muck and mud, we ain't faint-hearted, you know.

Me trusty 'orse and I, we're a blimey sight,
Bravin' the elements, ridin' in the pearly light.
With a stiff upper lip, me clobber drenched through,
Jacket soakin' wet, me boots all askew,

With me whip in hand, I guide 'er 'round the bend,
Splashin' through the slop, rain's ceaseless descend.
Rain lashing down like cats and dogs, it's true,
But we ain't no softies, me 'orse and me, we push through.

With each stride, we defy the weather's sneer,
Through puddles we prance, courage void of fear.
'Cause 'orses are me mates, standin' strong and tall,
Conquerin' the darkest storms, triumphin' overall.

So, here's to the noble steed, and to the cockney way,
Braving foul weather, come what may.
Embrace the elements, and don't you fret,
Ridin' in the awful weather, you won't ever forget.